NATIONAL GEOGRAPHIC

Ladders

LEND ME A PAW

Animals Can!

by Sara Hellwege

It's a busy day in the city. One worker patrols a park to keep it safe while another leads a blind person down a sidewalk. A third worker helps a patient in a hospital recover from an illness. What do the workers have in common? They are animals!

Therapy Animals

Friendly animals make many people smile. That's the idea behind animal **therapy.** Therapy is something that heals or helps people feel better, and therapy animals are animals that help people feel better. Therapy dogs and their owners visit hospitals and nursing homes. In many cases, patients' moods improve around a happy dog, and people who are stressed feel calm when they pet a dog's soft fur. Cats, rabbits, birds, and horses are also used as therapy animals.

A therapy horse visits senior citizens.

An animal needs the right **traits** to be a therapy animal. A trait is a quality that makes one thing different from another. Friendliness is a good trait for a therapy animal. Many dogs have this trait, and that's why dogs are the most common therapy animal. Other traits of therapy animals are listed below.

Traits of Therapy Animals

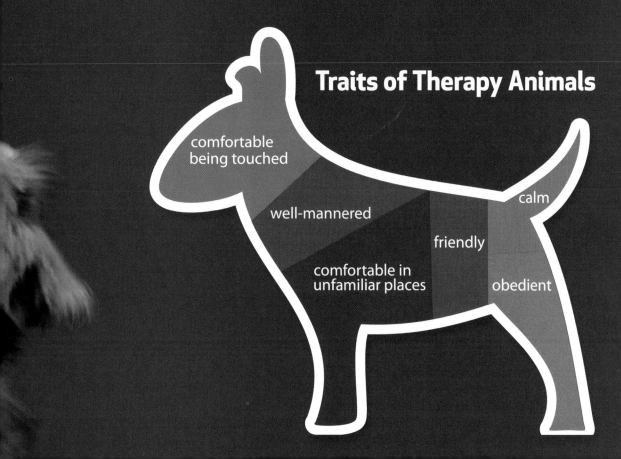

comfortable being touched

well-mannered

comfortable in unfamiliar places

friendly

calm

obedient

GOLDEN RETRIEVER
Job: search and rescue dog
Traits: keen sense of smell

Working Dogs

Some animals work for a living. Like traits, **instincts** are important for working animals. An instinct is a natural ability, and animals with certain instincts are good for certain jobs. Let's take a look at dogs. Because of their instincts, certain jobs come naturally to certain breeds of dogs.

Herding dogs have an instinct to gather and move livestock. In order to do their job well, herd dogs are trained and taught **commands.**

Search and rescue dogs rely on their instinct to hunt. They use this instinct to find people who are missing or trapped. A keen sense of smell is a trait that helps them do this. The dogs learn commands and are trained to follow a human scent. Then they're ready to work in emergency situations.

Guard dogs rely on their instinct to protect in order to keep people, places, and livestock safe. Strength and a loud, mean bark are traits that help guard dogs do their job. They are trained to use these instincts and traits to alert their owners and scare away intruders.

BORDER COLLIE
Job: herd dog
Traits: nimble, loud bark

GERMAN SHEPHERD
Job: guard dog
Traits: strong, stern bark

Service Animals

Service animals help people. A service animal is a dog that is trained to help a person with a **disability.**

- Guide dogs are service animals that help people who are blind get safely from place to place.

- Hearing dogs are service animals that help people who are deaf. They are trained to alert their owners to sounds and to lead them to the sound.

- Assistance dogs are service animals that help people with physical disabilities. They may pull someone in a wheelchair, pick up dropped items, or open doors.

LABRADOR RETRIEVER
Job: assistance dog
Traits: nimble, strong, instinctively helpful, intelligent

TERRIER
Job: hearing dog
Traits: alert, energetic, intelligent

According to U.S. law, service animals are allowed in public places, such as stores. This law is important because it gives service animals rights that other animals don't have. Service animals are working animals that wear a harness and a vest at work. If you see a service animal, you should follow a few simple rules:

- Talk to the person, not to the dog.

- Don't pet the dog unless you get permission. The dog is working. Petting or talking to it can distract it from its job.

LABRADOR RETRIEVER
Job: guide dog
Traits: calm, not easily distracted, intelligent

Beasts of Burden

A beast of burden has heavy work to do. A pack animal carries loads, a draft animal pulls loads, and some animals do both.

In the past, people used animals to do work. Today, animals are used if vehicles can't be used. Around the world, there are different beasts of burden, such as donkeys, oxen, water buffalo, reindeer, llamas, horses, elephants, yaks, and camels. Let's take a look at a few.

Asian elephants used to clear land and carry logs in Southeast Asia. Cutting down trees is now illegal in many countries. Some elephants and their handlers now patrol and protect forests.

In the Andes Mountains, llamas have transported goods for centuries. They still work as pack animals in places where cars and other vehicles can't go.

Camels carry heavy loads across the desert and walk up to 25 miles (40 kilometers) a day with little or no food and water.

The next time you see a furry, four-legged worker, stop. Remember that people and the vehicles we create can't do everything. Then say *thanks!*

An elephant moves a fallen tree in Thailand after the tsunami in 2004.

LLAMA
Job: pack animal
Traits: sure-footed in rocky, mountainous terrain
Location: Andes Mountains, South America

llama

ASIAN ELEPHANT
Job: pack animal and draft animal
Traits: strong, intelligent, flexible trunk
Location: India and Southeast Asia

BEASTS OF BURDEN

DROMEDARY CAMEL
Job: pack animal and draft animal
Traits: adapted for long-distance desert travel
Location: Northern Africa and the Middle East

camel

Check In What are some categories of working animals and what are the animals' traits and instincts?

9

Read to find out why dolphins and sea lions are used in this program instead of people.

The Navy Marine Mammal Program

by Shannae Wilson

In the "Navy **Marine Mammal** Program," bottlenose dolphins and California sea lions participate in U.S. military operations. These marine mammals have unique **traits.** These traits allow them to perform certain underwater tasks better than people or equipment can.

Sea lions and dolphins are excellent divers. They can dive deeper than people can. They can also dive more often and stay under water longer.

Sea lions have exceptional hearing and vision under water.

The animals follow **commands** to perform a variety of tasks. They protect ports, ships, and submarines against enemy swimmers. They also locate training equipment and sea mines. A sea mine is a weapon, like an underwater bomb. After the animals locate the objects, the Navy can remove or avoid them.

The animals can be transported to locations all over the world by ship, aircraft, or land vehicle. They have been used in past wars and conflicts.

People have different opinions about the Navy Marine Mammal Program. Some are in favor of the program (pro) and others are against it (con).

Sea lions and dolphins have an **instinct** to hunt under water.

Dolphins have a sense called **echolocation.** Echolocation allows them to locate objects. Manmade equipment is not nearly as effective at echolocation as dolphins.

Pro

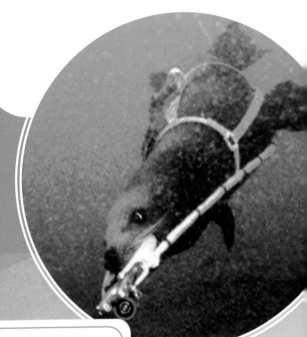

The Navy Marine Mammal Program should continue because it protects our troops. Also, it does not harm marine mammals. Here are three reasons why you should support it.

① First, more ships are damaged or destroyed by enemy sea mines than by any other cause. Dolphins and sea lions help prevent such disasters by locating sea mines.

② Secondly, it is unlikely that the animals will be harmed. Sea mines are not designed to be detonated by marine mammals.

③ Finally, the marine mammals are well cared for. The animals live in well-maintained enclosures, eat a balanced diet, and have regular physical exams by a veterinarian.

To protect our troops, we should continue the Navy Marine Mammal Program.

The Navy Marine Mammal Program puts marine mammals at risk. Here are three reasons why you should oppose it.

① First, it's not possible to provide the proper habitat for dolphins in captivity. In nature, dolphins travel up to 50 miles a day in open water. The Navy can't provide this habitat at all times.

② Secondly, the capture of dolphins from the wild is harmful. Dolphins live in social groups called *pods*. When they are captured, they are taken away from their pods. Also, some reports say that the capture of dolphins is exhausting and violent.

To protect marine mammals, we should end the Navy Marine Mammal Program.

③ Finally, war is a human problem. Animals are innocent and should not be made to participate. In the U.S., people have the choice to join the military or not to join. These animals do not have a choice.

Check In Which opinion do you agree with? Think about and state your reasons.

One Smart Dog

by Beth Finke

Beth

Harper

Beth writes in her home office. Harper helps!

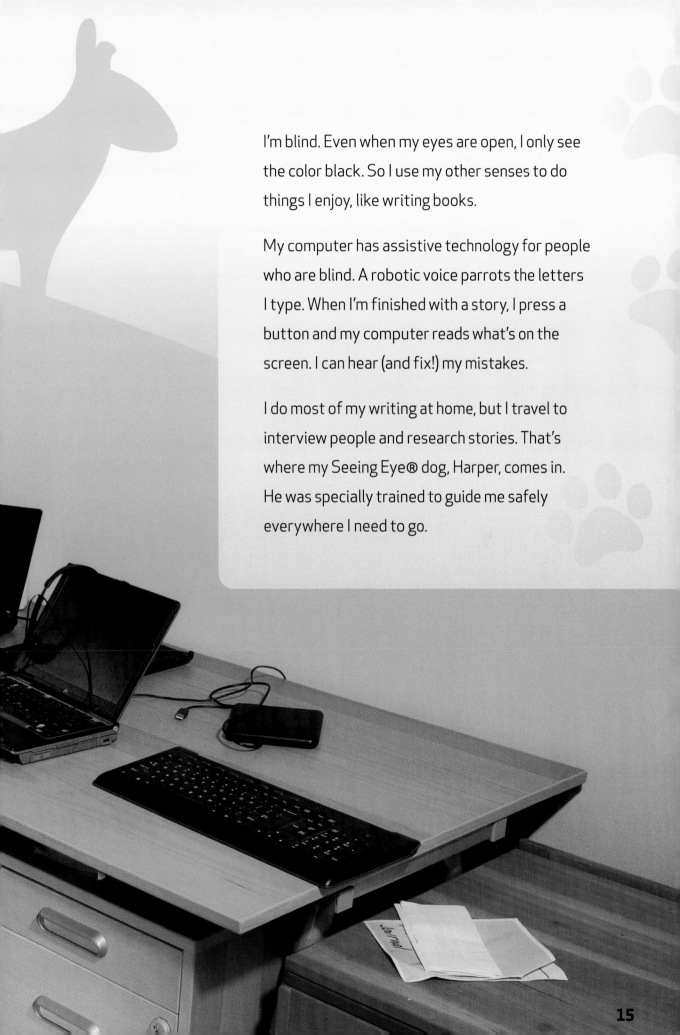

I'm blind. Even when my eyes are open, I only see the color black. So I use my other senses to do things I enjoy, like writing books.

My computer has assistive technology for people who are blind. A robotic voice parrots the letters I type. When I'm finished with a story, I press a button and my computer reads what's on the screen. I can hear (and fix!) my mistakes.

I do most of my writing at home, but I travel to interview people and research stories. That's where my Seeing Eye® dog, Harper, comes in. He was specially trained to guide me safely everywhere I need to go.

Seeing Eye School in Morristown, New Jersey

Harper was trained at the Seeing Eye School. Dozens of schools teach guide dogs to help people who are blind, but only guide dogs trained at the Seeing Eye school earn the official title "Seeing Eye dog." The Seeing Eye school breeds German Shepherds, Golden Retrievers, Labrador Retrievers, and mixes of these breeds. These breeds have **traits** that make them good guide dogs.

Golden Retriever mother and puppies

When Harper turned seven weeks old, he went to live with a volunteer, called a puppy raiser. Harper's puppy raiser taught him the basics: "sit" and "down," normal dog stuff. Harper's puppy raiser took him everywhere, exposing him to all sorts of people in all sorts of places.

Puppy raisers must take dogs to crowded places, like baseball games.

After his first birthday, Harper returned to the school. For four months, professional trainers spent every day teaching Harper to stop at stairs and at streets. Harper learned to judge traffic, and he was taught what "left" and "right" and "forward" mean.

Once Harper was ready, I flew to the Seeing Eye school to meet him. I fell in love with him the minute I saw (okay, touched!) him, and after practicing together for three weeks, I trusted Harper to keep me safe in traffic, so it was time to fly home.

Harper's ID card

OFFICIAL IDENTIFICATION

Ms. Beth Finke

and Seeing Eye® dog
HARPER

are graduates of The Seeing Eye
This card is not transferable.
Expires: **12/31/2013**

James A. Kutsch, Jr.

James A. Kutsch, Jr.
President

Harper is always eager to eat.

Harper waits until he gets a command.

Then he eats. Yum!

I feed and take care of Harper, and that's important because it helps build a bond between us. Every morning I scoop a cup of dog food, level it, and pour it into Harper's bowl. Then we get ready to go outside. Harper and I use two pieces of equipment: a harness that buckles around his chest with a sturdy handle for me to grab, and a leash. I clip on Harper's leash, buckle his harness and command, "Harper, forward!" When we get to at Harper's favorite tree, I unbuckle his harness so he knows it's okay to empty. (That's a polite word for *pee* and *poop*.)

Back home, I unbuckle Harper's harness and go to the kitchen sink. I lift his water bowl, and if it feels light, I know it's empty. I turn the water on and fill the bowl until it's heavy. I groom Harper every day, and when our workday is over we play tug-of-war and fetch with his favorite toys.

Beth uses a brush to groom Harper.

Harper loves to play.

19

Harper guides Beth across a street.

Good Dog!

Close your eyes. Imagine you can't see. Here's what you'd do to travel down a street with a Seeing Eye dog.

🐾 Lift the harness handle with your left hand.

🐾 Face the direction you want to go.

🐾 Say your dog's name and command, "Forward!"

🐾 Your dog will pull you forward.

🐾 When your dog stops, you stop, too.

🐾 Slide your foot forward to investigate why the dog stopped. Feel a curb, the top of the stairs? Praise your dog. He just saved you from falling.

Seeing Eye dogs fight their natural **instincts** to sniff, protect, and socialize while they're working. If Harper gets distracted by a squirrel zipping by, he might forget to stop at the curb.

And that's just the beginning. We still have to cross the street!

Dogs are color blind, so Harper can't tell if the stoplight is red or green. It's my job to judge when it's safe to cross. When it sounds like the traffic is going the direction I want to go, I guess that the light is green. "Harper, forward!" Harper's ears perk up, and he listens for traffic. Then he looks left and right to determine whether it's safe to pull me across.

If he thinks I've misjudged the traffic, or if he senses danger, Harper stays put. I can repeat the command and urge him forward. But Harper won't budge. Not until he's confident it's safe.

Let me tell you about **intelligent disobedience,** or refusing a command that is dangerous. Intelligent disobedience is the most difficult skill a Seeing Eye dog must learn. Harper uses intelligent disobedience in many situations. I'll leave you with a great example.

Harper and I were heading down a city sidewalk once when he stopped for no reason.

I felt ahead with my foot. Nothing there. I waved my arm in front of me. Nothing there either.

"Harper, forward!" I urged. I was in a hurry. Harper stood motionless.

"Right, right!" I tried. I hoped Harper might guide me around whatever he saw in the way. No luck.

Just then I heard a truck door slam. Heavy footsteps hurried toward us. "Watch out, ma'am! Stay put!" The truck driver offered his arm. "They just called me to come fix this door!" He guided us into the street for a bit, then led us back onto the sidewalk. "There's glass all over the place!"

The plate glass door had shattered. I couldn't have known this, but Harper did.

"That's one smart dog," our new friend told me. "Thanks," I agreed. "I think so, too!"

Harper watches for obstacles ahead.

That's one smart dog!

Discuss Text Structure, Details, and Examples

1. Describe how "Animals Can!" is organized. How does the organization help you compare information about the animals?

2. How are the opinions organized in "The Navy Marine Mammal Program"?

3. What reasons and evidence are presented to support the two differing opinions in "The Navy Marine Mammal Program"?

4. Think of an animal that you know, such as a pet. What kind of job would it be suited for? Explain why. Refer to details and examples from "Animals Can!"

5. What do you still wonder about working animals? What more would you like to find out?